AF357308

# Feeling All My Shyness

Kim T. S.

## Hi!

I was a shy kid and I used to feel bad about it. Others would comment about how quiet I was and how I should speak up more. I felt like something was wrong with me . . . so I pushed myself to change. This helped me do things I thought I couldn't, but it also led me to question my identity and made me feel ashamed of who I was.

It was only in adulthood that I learned to accept myself exactly as I am. What I thought of as weaknesses could be strengths if I learned to use them the right way!

I hope that kids can learn these lessons early on.

 Kim


Published by Kim T. S. - Doña Hemady St., Quezon City, Philippines
Rhyme & Meter Edits by RobinKatzEditor.com
www.kimtsbooks.com

To the shy kids: I see you and I
love you exactly as you are.

Meet Kayla! She's a quiet girl
who loves a cozy nook.
So, when she wants to be alone,
she curls up with a book.

Her friends are few and far between.
But love for her, they show.
It takes her time to open up—
Too shy to say "hello."

A lot of kids may feel that way.
It's perfectly okay.
There's nothing wrong with feeling shy,
no matter what they say.

Your feelings tend to come and go.
Just greet them and say hi.
Observe them as they visit you.
Then, learn to say goodbye.

When shyness keeps you from those things
you wish that you could do,
please ask for help from someone you
can trust to get you through.

You can't control how others feel
or what they think or say.
Try working on good ways to be
'a better you' each day.

No matter how you feel inside,
choose well what you will do.
You're stronger than you think you are.
You MUST believe that's true!

So, if you want to make new friends,
but feel unsure or shy,
remember. . . It gets easier
the more you bravely try.

Hi!

Some children never hesitate
to say what's on their mind.
Still others take more time to think . . .
'Cause that's how they're designed!

But in this hardened world, what's soft
may be misunderstood.
Some yearn for peace and listen first—
the way that people should.

We often notice fiery strength
explodes with quite a sound.
But water has a quiet power:
Gentle . . . yet profound.

You surely have a little bit
of both inside of you.
Explore your nature. Nurture it,
while 'To yourself, be true.'

And when you learn to love yourself,
that's when the magic starts.
Upholding all that you believe,
you'll touch so many hearts!

Throughout your life-long journey,
whether roaming near or far:
Remember that you're truly special . . .
Just the way you are!

Do you know that introversion is different from shyness?

# INTROVERSION MEANS:

You need time alone to recharge after being around lots of people

✓ You prefer small groups over large crowds

✓ You have few but very close friends

✓ You feel comfortable being alone

✓ You aren't afraid of talking to people

✓ You don't worry too much about being rejected by others

# SHYNESS MEANS:

You feel nervous, afraid, awkward, or tense around others, especially unfamiliar people.

- ✓ You want to talk to people but you avoid it
- ✓ You focus on what others think of you
- ✓ You worry a lot about being rejected by others

It's normal to feel shy sometimes! But if it causes you distress, there are ways to overcome it.

 Everyone has things they are good at and things they need to work on! That makes us human.

# MY STRENGTHS ARE:

Example: I am a good listener. I think before I speak. I am kind. I am thoughtful. I easily understand how others feel.

# THINGS I CAN IMPROVE ON:

Example: I won't worry too much about what others think.
Stop comparing myself to others. Focus on improving myself.
I can do hard things no matter how I feel.

# NOT EVERYONE WILL LIKE YOU, AND THAT'S OKAY.

Everyone wants to be liked. But you can't expect everyone to like you, just as others can't expect you to like everyone.

No matter how you feel about someone, it's important to be kind. If others are unkind to you, you can stand up for yourself or simply walk away.

# JUST BE YOURSELF.

There are people who will like you exactly the way you are. They are the ones who should matter most to you!

Believe in yourself, but be open to feedback from others. No one is perfect! We're all learning and growing.

# DO YOU WORRY TOO MUCH ABOUT WHAT OTHERS THINK OF YOU?

Here's a secret: Most people think of themselves more than they think of you!

You can't control what others think but you can control how you act and react.

Try not to take yourself too seriously. You can learn to shake or laugh it off!

What YOU think is just as important as what others think. Your opinion matters.

Be kind to yourself. How would you talk to a friend in the same situation?

It's okay to fail. It means you tried something new and you are learning.

# MISTAKES ARE A NORMAL PART OF LIFE!

When you become "good" at making mistakes and at failing, you won't let fear stop you from trying again and again!

Think of a time when you made a mistake.
What did you learn from it?
How can you do better next time?

What is one thing you've been feeling too shy to try? How can you prepare yourself to do it?

# LIFE IS ABOUT BALANCE

Too much of anything can be harmful.

Too much **SHYNESS** can stop you from doing what you love.

Too much **CONFIDENCE** can stop you from preparing for risks.

Too much **FEAR** can make you feel powerless and stuck.

Too much **BRAVERY** can get you hurt.

# STOP COMPARING YOURSELF TO OTHERS

Would you judge a fish by how well it can climb a tree? You are different from everyone else and are on your own unique journey. Focus on improving yourself!

# CHANGE "WHAT IF" TO "EVEN IF"

"Even if they don't like me . . .
I will find someone who does."
"Even if I fail . . . I will learn from it."

# Want freebies?

Get FREE emotional regulation activity sheets through our mailing list. Use your smartphone camera to scan the code below, then tap the link. Or visit our website!

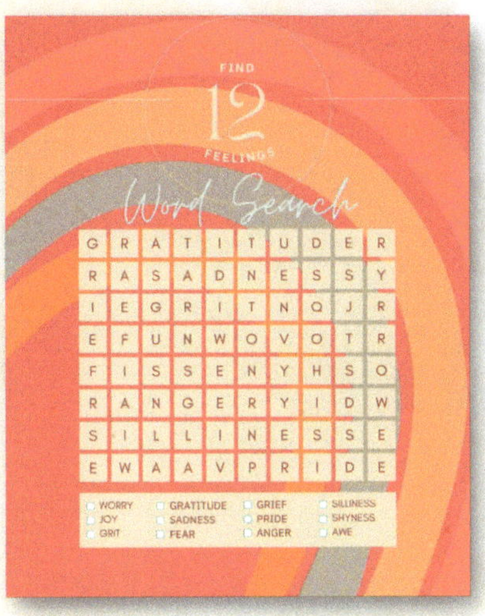

@kimt.s.books - @kimtsbooks - kimtsbooks@gmail.com

# www.kimtsbooks.com